SORROW LIKE
NO OTHER

St. Jude Children's®
Research Hospital

Finding cures. Saving children.
ALSAC · DANNY THOMAS, FOUNDER

stjude.org/givehope

healingjourney@
ctcemeteries.org

2A1

SORROW LIKE NO OTHER

Supporting the Grief of Parents Whose Child Has Died

CHARLEY and DIANE
MONAGHAN

SORROW LIKE NO OTHER
Supporting the Grief of Parents Whose Child Has Died
Charley and Diane Monaghan

Editing by Gregory F. Augustine Pierce
Cover and text design and typesetting by Andrea Reider

Published by ACTA Publications, Chicago, IL 60640,
(800) 397-2282, www.actapublications.com

ISBN: 978-0-87946-719-7
Library of Congress Catalog number: 2022939793
Printed in the United States of America by Total Printing
Systems
Year 30 29 28 27 26 25 24 23 22
Printing 10 9 8 7 6 5 4 3 2 First
Text printed on 30% post-consumer recycled paper

CONTENTS

Introduction

What Gives
Us Comfort

THE GRIEF OF A PARENT who has lost a child, is unlike any other type of grief. Grieving parents who have also lost spouses, parents, siblings, best friends—without exception—say that the loss of a child is a very different type of grief. Why is this so?

The death of a child—no matter how old (from before birth to any age, because a child is always a child and a parent is always a parent), or how they died (from illness, pandemic, accident, crime violence, war, miscarriage, abortion, overdose, addiction, suicide)—is out of the natural order. In addition to their precious child, parents also lose their future hopes and dreams for that child. At the same time, they often also experience significant destabilization of their families and their marriages. Recent studies published by the National Institute of Health have concluded that the death of a child is the most devastating and stressful of any life event.[1]

After the death of a child, for a time, many parents are so affected by their grief that they are unable to focus and concentrate as they did before the death. As one parent said, "After a year, I was still unable to read any news but headlines."

For many grieving parents, things that seemed so important before now hold no meaning. A total reevaluation of life is not uncommon. Many, if they are able, quit their jobs to pursue something that seems now more meaningful. Some adopt causes to honor their children. Others continue to search for ways to make sense of what has happened, often to no avail. At a minimum, most grieving parents have little patience for "chit chat" or inconsequential conversations or activities.

The death of a child very often reveals a profound truth about friendships. People you thought were your friends are definitely not there for you; suddenly, you have nothing in common. "After the death of a child," one parent said, "you need to rewrite your address book." That being said, it is not unusual for God to place new friends and new opportunities for growth in your life.

Most grieving parents are no longer afraid of death. Some even feel a compelling need to try to find their children in the afterlife through seances or mediums, just to be assured they are OK. Others even look forward to joining their child in death because they see no reason for living. These are both natural human responses, but parents who have suffered this "pain unlike

3

any other" need to be reminded that the death of their child does not mean that they are no longer parents. That is the purpose of this little book. We can still minister to our children by praying for them, by living a life they would be proud of, and by dedicating our lives for good. We believe that someday all parents can and will join their children in heaven. That is our very real hope for ourselves, and this book will try to make that same hope true for you as well.

God make it so. Amen.

Charley and Diane Monaghan
Paul's Parents
Boston, Massachusetts
On the 20th Anniversary of Paul's Death, 2022

Why is the grief of a parent whose child has died like no other?

MARIA GOT TO STARBUCKS early one morning for coffee with us. As soon as she sat down, we could see that she was visibly upset.

"What's the matter, Maria?" we asked her. She replied, "On my way here, I saw Denita. I couldn't believe what she said to me. She said, 'How are you, Maria?' How could she say that to me? How could she ask me how I am? Does she not know how sad I am after the death of my son? I can't believe how insensitive people can be."

Irrational? Yes. Unusual? No, not for a parent whose child has died. These kinds of simple, innocuous questions or innocent statements may have caused no problem before the death of a child, but now they can cause immense and searing pain. And the people making these statements are clueless this is happening.

Examples of such thoughtless statements by well-meaning people include:

- "How many (other) children do you have?" (Innocent, yet hurtful, question for grieving parents who struggle with how to answer it.)
- "He/she is in a better place." (I don't want him to be in a better place. I want him to be here with me.)
- "Are you getting over it?" (I'll never be over it.)
- "At least you can have more children." (What child could possibly substitute for

the child I have lost, even if we can have another child?)

- "At least you had her/him for xx years." (What year of life would you choose for *your* child to die?)
- Perhaps this one is the hardest: "I know what you are going through." (Unless you are a fellow grieving parent, you really *don't* know what the grieving parent is going through.)

II

How long is the duration and intensity of a parent's grief?

WE FIND THAT DURATION and intensity of grief can differ among parents. Some who have witnessed their child suffer—from a prolonged illness, a lengthy addiction, etc.—tell us that they suffered the most during their child's ordeal. The death may have brought a sense of calm and relief, but this is always accompanied by an aching loneliness and sometimes guilt at something else they "should have" or "could have" or "wish they had" done.

Other parents have told us that their encounter with grief was delayed for some period of time. They say that being so engrossed in holding the funeral, setting up arrangements for visiting relatives, and ministering to their other children and spouse, as well as needy grand-parents, aunts, uncles, and others put them in a fog. They can't even remember what actually happened. We have been told that going on one of our Emmaus retreats (see "About the Authors") was, for some, the release they had never experienced until that moment.

For most, however, the grief of the death of their child is immediate and intense. This is typically when the Church steps in to minister with consolation and assistance. However, a common refrain that we hear is that after the initial consolation the Church community, the pastor or pastoral associates, even the other parishioners retire into the background and seem to assume that life for the grieving parent has returned to "normal" and that they're doing OK.

For most parents, this is the farthest thing from the truth. In fact, the grief seems to intensify because there is always a period of time before the true ramifications of the death of their child become evident to parents. We theorize that this is because of the part shock plays in the process. For us, our son's death was so unexpected that we believe that the only way that we were able to function as employed adults for the first year was that God gave us the numbing gift of shock, as God often seems to do so for other grieving parents as well.

In time, however, the shock wears off. This is when the lifelong journey of grief work begins. At many of our retreats, a parent whose loss was recent will ask, "How long does it last before it gets any better?" With no prompting from us, another parent with will inevitably express their view that the second year of the child's passing was the worst (as indeed it was for us). That's because on the second Thanksgiving, the second Christmas, the second birthday, etc., it dawns upon you: "This is the way it is always going to be from now on. Our life will never be as it was before! Our beautiful child is never coming home." The fog is lifted and the reality finally hits you.

In time, however, the sharp pain does indeed subside. You begin to learn to live with the dull constant ache. However, almost every parent has triggers that can return them to uncontrolled grief and pain. It may be that you're walking in a mall and a song comes over the music system that you equate with a memory of your child. Perhaps you see a sports fan wearing a jersey of your son's alma mater or favorite team. Or you watch a mother walking hand in hand with her very cute little girl. In no time, you're rushing into a restroom or your parked car, sobbing uncontrollably or just emotionally numb.

The triggers differ and are as varied and inexplicable as human beings themselves. For example, shortly after our son, Paul, died, we moved to a high-rise condo building in Boston. For at least the first five years we were there, we recoiled at getting into the elevator with any family bringing young children to visit. Even though Paul reached adulthood, he was always our blue-eyed, blond-haired, little boy. As a couple, we never discussed these moments with each other, yet we discovered recently we had both been having the same reaction to sharing an elevator with a family with a child who looked like our Paul. It made no sense then or now, but elevators were nonetheless a real trigger of deep pain for the two of us for a long time.

As another example, since our son passed, the New England Patriots have won five Super Bowls, the Boston Red Sox broke an 89-year drought and won three World Series, and the Boston Celtics and Bruins have each won a championship. Yet I (Charley) have enjoyed none of them and generally avoided watching the games because Paul was passionate about Boston sports and, as he wasn't here to enjoy these triumphs with me, neither could I.

Almost all grieving parents we have met have shared that they have experienced similar irrational triggers. We believe that those who minister with them need to be aware of this phenomenon.

III

Do parents progress through the so-called "stages of grief"?

IN OUR EXPERIENCE and that of most parents we've companioned, we answer a resounding "NO!" to this question.

We've found that our lived grief experience is not linear. Many grieving parents tell of finding themselves returning without warning to guilt, anger, shock, and other emotions even after years have passed since their child died. As the old song goes: "Some days are diamonds, some days are stones"—and we grieving parents never know which it will be…or why. The "stages of grief" formula implies that you just need to go through the steps correctly and then the grieving process will be over for you.

This is not what we and most other parents experience over the death of our child, though many professionals believe we are just not facing the truth. But we know how and what we feel.

IV

What feelings are common among parents who've lost a child?

A MAJORITY OF PARENTS begin their grief journey with an intense search for answers. We suggest that this need stems from the great spiritual battle that rages around us, and that the Great Accuser (however you name or think about the power of evil) uses all these feelings as offensive tactics against us.

We've found that almost every parent wrestles with reconciling the question of "*Why?*" It can be framed as: "Why did God take my child?" or "Why were my prayers not answered?" or "Why did God do this to me?" Then there are also the questions of "*Where?*" This is articulated this way: "Where was God when I needed God?" or "Where is my child now?" These seem to be foundational questions that each parent must confront before making any sense in their grief journey.

Flowing from these feelings, perhaps, many parents need to have someone, anyone, to blame and direct their anger towards. The most obvious and readily acceptable target is God. In addition to the "*Why*" questions, anger at God typically begins from trying to reconcile the notion of an all-loving God with the pain an all-powerful God has either caused or permitted or was unable to prevent. For many, this difficulty alone causes them to discard any relationship with God. If it's not God, other initial targets sometimes prove even more useful: the driver of the other car, the doctor whose surgery didn't work, the dealer that supplied the drugs, etc.

We humans seem to find comfort in wrapping ourselves in righteous anger so that deeper feelings or issues of our own don't have to be confronted. We do find, however, that—although the period of overcoming anger at the death of a child can be lengthy—we seldom find many parents who are permanently trapped in their anger. It's hard work to be angry all the time. This may be because someone permanently simmering in anger would not participate in a ministry program like the ones we run, but we think it is more universal than that. We suspect it simply takes too much emotional energy to remain permanently in a state of anger. Having said that, we do find that most parents can temporarily return to anger almost as a crutch.

Anger needs an object—someone or something—to be directed towards. Sometimes, when there's no obvious object, people will direct it towards themselves. We've encountered many parents who are trapped in the inward struggle of the eternal woulda-shoulda-coulda syndrome with debilitating effects. This kind of self-directed anger seems to be easier to sustain than that aimed at God or others; we've companioned parents who have dealt with these self-directed feelings for decades. In certain instances, they've applied blame to the other parent involved, with separation or divorce almost always the result.

Almost every parent who loses a child is permanently scarred and changed. Activities, events, and people who once had meaning now seem to require too much effort to deal with. Former friends or relatives avoid you, or perhaps never again mention your child, either because they don't know what to say or don't want to offend or upset you. This, instead, reinforces the feeling of being alienated and totally alone.

Finally, most parents tell of their exhaustion and resentment at having to "act normal" 24/7 when really they are in great internal upheaval.

V

What feelings are common to grieving mothers?

A GOOD DESCRIPTION of what a grieving mother feels, I (Diane) believe, is found in this poem:

The Invisible Cord

We are connected, my child and I,
by an invisible cord not seen by the eye

It's not like the cord that connects us 'til birth,
This cord can't be seen by any on Earth

This cord does its work right from the start
It binds us together, attached to my heart

I know that it's there, though no one can see
The invisible cord from my child to me

The strength of this cord is hard to describe
It can't be destroyed, it can't be denied

It's stronger than any cord man could create
it withstands the test, can hold any weight

And though you are gone, and not here with me
The cord is still there, but no one can see

It pulls at my heart, I am bruised, I am sore
But this cord is my lifeline as never before

I am thankful that God connects us this way
A mother and child, death can't take it away!

Author Unknown

Whether you are a birth mother or adoptive mother, the special bond you have with your child can never be broken, even by death. Studies have shown that mothers continue to carry particles of their children's DNA in their bodies for decades, or even longer. According to a study published in Clinical Chemistry in 2020, "The lifelong exchange of cells between a mother and her child is profound…. This intricate exchange of genetically foreign cells creates a permanent connection."[2]

For us grieving mothers, "The presence of their absence is everywhere." The more you love, the more you hurt. The hole in your heart can be debilitating, especially in the beginning. It will heal only in the next life, when you and your child are together again.

Because the loss of a child is so traumatic, parents can develop physical manifestations of their grief, including cancer[3] and heart problems.[4]

It is often comforting for parents to think that the part of a mother's heart (the hole that is no longer there) is now in heaven. Therefore, she doesn't need to search for it, because she knows some day she will be reunited with it.

VI

~~~~~~~

What feelings are common to grieving fathers?

GUILT. THAT'S WHAT I (Charley) felt. So many men see their role as protector of the family as their identity. When their child dies, regardless of when or how, they get the nagging feeling that they failed to protect someone they were supposed to protect.

Men also seem to have been molded by the culture to accept that to be a man is to be strong, stoic, and unemotional. They often suppress their

own feelings so that they can comfort their wives
and other children. I can't speak for all men, but
I will say that although I accepted this image of
myself, I was never emotionally prepared for it.
When experiencing the "sorrow like no other" of
the death of a child, men are often afraid to show
or talk about what they're feeling for fear their
façade will collapse and they'll be seen as "weak."
Consequently, we men clam up and attempt to
put all recollection of our child and what the child
meant to us out of our minds and not deal with it.
During one period of time in my life, I often said,
"I have Paul in a box, and I'm not taking him out."

The death of a child is outside of the natural
order. Parents should not be burying children,
so many of us feel we must have done something
wrong. There is tremendous guilt in thinking,
"How could I have squandered such a beautiful
gift? Why didn't I die instead of my child? Will
God ever forgive me? Will my spouse/other
children ever forgive me? Is there any hope for my
family's future?"

VII

How does the loss of a child challenge a grieving couple?

A TYPICAL MAXIM WITHIN the marriage partnership is: "We're in this together." Thus, many couples expect that they should grieve together, in the same way, and at the same time. This is not possible, as grief is an individual journey; the sexes grieve very differently; and none of us have the exact same feelings at the exact same time. This puts tremendous stress on the marriage.[1]

We frequently hear from wives about their husband: "He won't talk about it" or "He won't deal with it" or, vice versa, "She never smiles" or "She won't quit crying." This leads to frustration with and even bitterness toward each other.

Some spouses innately feel the need to "fix" things. This instinct often adds a seemingly insurmountable level of pain or resentment. In time, this can lead to a point where one or both of the spouses gives up on the relationship. Many marriages have trouble coping with this exact issue, but it is greatly exacerbated with the death of a child.

If the child's death was the result of an accident that also involved one or both parents, this can put an incredible burden of anger and guilt on the entire family. Parents and often siblings may need intensive pastoral counseling on the freedom that comes from forgiveness. Seeking help early is essential in this situation.

VIII

How can the loss of a child affect a parent's relationship with remaining (or future) children?

THE DEATH OF ONE'S SIBLING can be a complicated issue in itself. We've had children express their resentment at being the "forgotten mourner" as compassion from others seems to be directed exclusively towards their parents, while their own grief many times are unnoticed.

The remaining child or children, regardless of maturity, can either sense or see that there's something very different about mom or dad; but they too have not only lost a brother or sister who was a huge part of their family. They eventually begin to long for life to return to normal, but it doesn't. In extreme cases, the child may begin to believe that they are less loved by their parents than the deceased child is.

The remaining child or children, regardless of maturity, can either sense or see that there's something very different about Mom and/or Dad. Siblings have not only lost a brother or sister, whom they loved very much and who was a huge part of their family, but they also sometimes feel they have lost a huge part of their parents that is never coming back.

Siblings eventually begin to long for life to return to normal, but it doesn't. In extreme cases, the child may begin to believe that they are less loved by their parents than the deceased child is.

IX

What is the special bond all grieving parents share?

IN WALKING WITH grieving parents over the years, we have found that the bond they share with one another, even when meeting for the first time, is almost instantaneous and very deep. Instinctively, they know when someone else "gets it." There is a real sense of relief when this happens

It doesn't matter the age of their children at death—or how they died—the immediate connection between grieving parents is strong. This is because their pain is so deeply shared. The only difference is the specifics of the deaths and the range of emotions they are each experiencing at the time they meet.

In our experience, this immediate connection is not always there between those suffering from other losses, such as a parent, a sibling, a neighbor, a best friend. Those morning such losses need to be addressed, but perhaps apart from and differently than those who have lost a child.

X

What do grieving parents need?

MORE THAN ANYTHING ELSE, grieving parents need hope that their children are still alive. They need peace in knowing they will be together with their child again someday. And they need comfort from their faith, family, and ministers or friends who understand the nature of their grief.

In addition, grieving parents need validation of whatever they are feeling, as long as it is not destructive. Mostly, that is the acknowledgement that the pain of a grieving parent is unlike any other sorrow—and that the pain is not going to go away. Parents can work through their grief, but they won't ever "get over" it. The term "closure" is not helpful in this situation.

XI

For those ministering to grieving parents

- Ask us to tell you about our children. Encourage us to talk about them—a lot. One of our biggest fears is that our children may be forgotten or treated as if they never existed. We need to hear people say their names out loud. We need other people who knew them to tell us about their memories of our children. If we feel comfortable that you are truly compassionate and interested, most of us *do* want to talk about our children and what we are going through.

As one parent said of his daughter, "Her memory is sustained through speaking about her and our feelings about her death. Deny this and you deny her life. Deny her life and you have no place in ours. That's the equation."[5] Harsh, but true for many parents.

- Don't be afraid to sit quietly and let us cry. Crying is therapeutic, not detrimental. Studies have shown that the DNA of tears of grief is very different from tears of joys, cutting onions, etc. Tears of grief contain toxins that the body needs to release through crying. This is one reason why grieving parents need to cry so much and why crying should actually be encouraged. No one ever died from crying.[6]

- Although you may have experienced the loss of a parent, spouse, or sibling, acknowledge that you have no idea of what we are feeling. Instead, offer to walk beside us as we grieve, no matter what. Remind us over and over again of our rich Catholic teachings: "Life has changed, not ended. It is possible to have a relationship with your child now; you don't have to wait until you die. Someday there will be a glorious reunion and you will all be together again. You will definitely hug and kiss your child again."

- Refer to our children in the present tense based on your belief in the promise of eternal life. It is empowering to a grieving parent to hear someone else speak of their child this way. The body may have died, but the soul lives on forever. For example, ask "What *is* your child's name?" not "What *was* your child's name?"
- Avoid judging our grief, because many of our feelings can seem irrational. Grieving parents simply need you to validate our

feelings. As long as our reactions are not destructive, almost anything a grieving parent feels, especially in the beginning of our grief journey, is acceptable.

- Many people believe that a certain period of time is "long enough" to grieve and that our grief should be over or significantly gone. This usually is not true with grieving parents. Eventually we won't act as if it happened yesterday, but grieving parents don't get over our grief. With the help of our faith, family, and friends, we get *through* it, one step at a time, every day, for the rest of our lives here on Earth. We are sustained by our belief that we will be reunited again with our dead children in Heaven. Respect and allow us to hold on to that belief. If you share that belief, let us know that. If not, just hold our hand.

XII

Ways local parishes or congregations most effectively support grieving parents

- They recognize the need for both immediate and ongoing bereavement ministry for those who have lost a child.
- They create specific ministry programs for the deaths of children, including appropriate funeral services; All Soul's Day remembrances; ways of remembering anniversaries of children's deaths and birthdays; other special events.
- They conduct ongoing support groups for parents that include spiritual

nourishment (e.g., our Emmaus Ministry retreats for grieving parents); special Masses; other programs.

- They host communal meals specifically for grieving parents. We've heard many times at our retreats how much parents appreciate sharing a meal while laughing, crying, and talking at ease about one another's children. They tell us they never get an opportunity to do this anywhere else.

- They recognize the needs of segmented grief support for parents separate from those grieving the loss of a spouse, a sibling, a parent, a neighbor, a friend.

Notes

[1] Catherine H. Rogers, Frank J. Floyd, Marsha Mailick Seltzer, Jan Greenberg, and Jinkuk Hong. "Long-Term Effects of the Death of a Child on Parents' Adjustment in Midlife." Journal of Family Psychology. April, 2008. https://pubmed.ncbi.nlm.nih.gov/18410207/#:~:text=An%20average%20of%2018.05%20years,disruption %20than%20were%20comparison%20parents.

[2] Diane W Bianchi, Kiarash Khosrotehrani, Sin Sin Way, Tippi C MacKenzie, Ingeborg Bajema, Keelinn O'Donoghue. "Forever Connected: The Lifelong Biological Consequences of Fetomaternal and Maternofetal Microchimerism." Clinical Chemistry. December 17, 2020. https://academic.oup.com/clinchem/article/67/2/351/6071463

[3] Jiong Li, Christoffer Johansen, Dorthe Hansen, Jern Olsen. "Cancer Incidence in Parents Who Lost a Child: A Nationwide Study in Denmark". Cancer Journal. November 15, 2002. https://acsjournals.onlinelibrary. wiley.com/doi/10.1002/cncr.10943

[4] Nicholas Bakalar, "The Loss of a Child Takes a Physical Toll on the Heart." The New York Times. November 23, 2021. https://www.nytimes. com/2021/11/23/well/family/death-of-a-child-parents-heart-attack-risk.html

[5] Michael Crelinsten. *My Journey Through Grief: The Gap.* Blogspot.com. February 13, 2010. http://myjour-neythroughgrief.blogspot.com/2010/02/gap.html

[6] Jennifer Stern, LISW. *Tears: Transformative Grief.* December 1, 2017. https://transformativegrief. com/2017/12/01/tears/

About the Authors

ON THANKSGIVING NIGHT in 2002, our beautiful son Paul, who lived on a military base 2000 miles away from us, died by suicide with no warning and for no apparent reason. The next night, three Air Force officers waited for hours in our driveway for us to come home from dinner so that they could give us the most devastating news anyone can give to another human being. In an instant, life as we knew it changed forever.

After many years of darkness and despair, finally we found hope. Hope in the rich teachings of the Catholic Church that life, for Paul, has *changed*, not ended. Hope in the fact that we will see him again. Hope in the fact that he is still alive and well and active in our lives every day.

Our faith, especially the promise of eternal life, brought us so much peace and comfort that in 2009 we felt called to dedicate the rest of our lives to bringing this same peace and comfort to other grieving parents that we have received from the teachings of the Catholic Church. With the Franciscan Friars of Holy Name Province at St. Anthony Shrine in Boston, Massachusetts, we founded the Emmaus Ministry for Grieving Parents.

The entire focus of this ministry is to provide the opportunity for parents to concentrate on their *spiritual* journeys, to grow closer to God and to their children. We are not holistic in that we do not attempt to serve all mind, body, and social needs. We believe that in serving the spiritual needs of grieving parents we are serving the most important need—that which will bring the true peace and comfort that grieving parents need most.

To this day, through Half-Hour, One-Hour, One-Day, and Weekend Spiritual Retreats (both in-person and virtual), the Emmaus Ministry continues to serve the spiritual needs of parents whose children of any age have died by any cause no matter how long ago. Since the founding of this ministry, we have led close to 200 retreats and have accompanied more than 2500 grieving parents in their journey of grief.

In doing so, we have found the experiences we have described in this book to be very common, either in total or in part, to most grieving parents with whom we have interacted. Occasionally we have encountered a parent, who is so spiritually and emotionally grounded that they have encountered few of the feelings we describe, though these parents are definitely the exception. One thing we have come to know for sure is that the sorrow of a parent whose child has died is unlike any other.

When grieving parents come to an Emmaus Ministry spiritual retreat, they are giving themselves the gift of getting away from everyday life to focus on where God is in their lives right now. They are not coming to a workshop or seminar, group therapy, or counseling. They are coming to a spiritual retreat, a way to recharge their spiritual lives.

We listen to other parents share their stories and give witness to their own spiritual journeys after the death of their children. However, no one is forced to say anything. Many people participate by listening, and that is perfectly acceptable at an Emmaus retreat. We gather together in small groups of mothers and fathers to talk about what we are feeling at that particular time and how mothers and fathers sometimes grieve differently.

We write letters to our children (or to God or to someone else), saying things we never said before; things we wished we would have said; things we wish we would not have said; things that we are feeling right now; things we could never tell anyone else. Later on in the retreat we offer these letters up in prayer as burnt ash.

During our Emmaus Walk, we invoke the Holy Spirit to pair us. We walk (or sit) with each other one-on-one to share our stories. The result is usually a very moving encounter with another grieving parent, with whom we will always thereafter have a special bond.

As we parents focus on our spiritual journeys throughout these retreats, the presence of the Holy Spirit—and the presence of our children— often becomes very palpable. Throughout the day, there is an overwhelming feeling of peace, comfort, and hope.

Many people, when hearing of a whole day or weekend retreat focused on grief, believe that this must be a very depressing and gloomy experience. Past Emmaus Retreat participants, however, without exception, say that it is very much a day of hope, not sadness. A day of peace, reaffirming our belief that someday we will be together with our children again. And a day of comfort, knowing that we are not alone in our sadness.

For more information on the Emmaus Ministry for Grieving Parents and our programs, visit www.emfgp.org, email info@emfgp.org, or call Diane Monaghan at 800-919-9332.

Books on Loss and Grief

- *An A-Z Guide to Letting Go; Constructing a New Normal;* and *Prayers for Difficult Times* by Helen Reichert Lambin
- *Born to Fly: An Infant's Journey to God* by Cindy Claussen
- *Catholic and Mourning a Loss: 5 Challenges and 5 Opportunities for Catholics to Live and Mourn through a Loss* by Mauryeen O'Brien
- *First Tears after the Loss of Your Child* by Linda Anderson
- *An Empty Space in Your Heart: Reflections on the Death of a Sibling or Best Friend* by Helen Reichert Lambin; *Death of a Child* by Elaine Stillwell; *Death of a Husband* by Helen Reichert Lambin, *Death of a Parent* by Delle Chapman; and *Death of a Wife* by Robert Vogt
- *A Gathering of Angels: Seeking Healing after an Infant's Death* by Victoria Leland, Linda Bailey, and Audra Fox-Murphy
- *God Shed His Grace on Thee: Moving Remembrances of 50 American Catholics* compiled by Carol DeChant (also available on CD)

Available from booksellers or
www.actapublications.com or 800-397-2282

Books on Loss and Grief

- *Grieving with Mary* by Mary K. Doyle
- *A Healing Year: Daily Meditations for Living with Loss* by Alaric Lewis
- *The Healing Garden: A Catalyst for Hope in Cicago* by Michael Hoffman and Fr. Larry Dowling
- *Hidden Presence: Twelve Blessings That Transformed Sorrow or Loss* compiled by Gregory F. Augustine Pierce
- *Someone Came before You;* and *We Were Gonna Have a Baby, but We Had an Angel Instead* by Pat Schwiebert, illustrated by Taylor Bills
- *Sorrow Like No Other: Supporting the Grief of Parents Whose Child Has Died* by Charley and Diane Monaghan
- *Tear Soup: A Recipe for Healing After Loss* by Pat Schweibert and Chuck DeKlyen, illustrated by Taylor Bills (also available in Spanish)
- *To Say a Few Words: Guidelines for Those Offering Words of Remembrance at a Roman Catholic Funeral* by Michael Cymbala

Available from booksellers or
www.actapublications.com or 800-397-2282